Coffee &

Chocolate

Skin

BY: Robert Lee Wilson III

ISBN: 9781658344869

Printed in the United States of America

I would like to give a special thanks to all the Beautiful Black Women in my life.
This book was inspired and dedicated to all of you.
And a special thanks to Brandon Williams for the amazing cover illustration.

Coffee and Chocolate Skin

I found myself drinking coffee while trying to trace the origins of her Chocolate coated skin. Like an astrologist searching the stars for an answer; I was searching her body for a sign of divinity. She was alone in a bookstore where melanated authors graced the bookshelves with their black excellence. As she continued to browse the inventory of remarkable books, I began to wonder what her position on life is? Does she have an idea of politics within a world full of politicians? Has she ever been in love, currently searching or presently enjoying a lover's bliss? I casually spark up a conversation and ask, "Do you like poetry?" And to my surprise, she replied "Yes!" So, I insisted she read *"If Poetry Were Short Stories"* the Author tells stories through poetry and in his latest collection *"Coffee and Chocolate Skin"* he writes about his love and admiration for black women and other topics as well. She smiled, we laughed and talked for what seemed to be hours. The entire time she had a glow I couldn't escape. Her skin was dark and reminded me of a chocolate velvet cake, and I was drawn to her smile like a deer in headlights. Who was this Melanated Queen who stood before me? What have I done to be so blessed with her presence? She had a glow like the Sun was born from her radiance and the Moon was jealous, so she shared it between the two of them. If today was the day the Earth stood still, my world would keep revolving. Her gravitational pull had me in her orbit and this must be what love at first sight feels like. I wonder... is this the meaning of *"The 8th Sin of Poetry"* and if so, let the story begin.

Find Yourself

You look like you taste of honey and brown sugar
With swirls of the world's finest chocolate
You smell like the purest of cinnamon sticks
Yet you are discouraged by the way society sees you
You've been kissed by the Sun and blessed with his radiance
Your voice is the sweetest song next to a hummingbird on a Sunday morning
But you feel as if your mahogany skin has been a blessing and a curse to you
But honestly, I'll kiss a sparrow or dance with a spider just to have you in my residence
And I apologize on behalf of all my black brothers' negligence
It's hard to believe someone so beautiful can feel so tragic
Tell me love, what happened to your black girl magic
Did you let the world steal your power
Did not receiving the love you were giving put you in a weakened state of mind
You were born to rule the land
What happened to that girl that was going to save this world one day at a time
What happened to the girl that chased Fireflies in the Spring
Just to slay Dragons during the Summer
In order to create peace in the Fall, because we all know that Winter is coming
And what happened to the girl that loves to go on adventures and discover new wonders
What happened to that joy

Find yourself and don't let history repeat itself
Love yourself and be free
Open your Angel wings and discover your inner being
Blow the dust off your halo and adjust your Crown
Queen
Let me hear you sing that you always remember why
the caged bird sings

If these Blues could cry

If these Blues could smile
I wouldn't worry about where you are
And if these blues could smile
I wouldn't be wishing upon distant stars
Praying to a God who won't answer my cries
Lying to myself for a woman who can't pick a side
Why must I try to run and hide and not realize
That I can't make my blues smile
All they do is cry
My blue skies don't hear lullabies
I'm deaf to the sound of love
Because these blues won't smile
I feel the walls closing and I'm losing time
My heart knows pain and my mind feels the same
I hate feeling this way because Blue isn't my color
I should've made better decisions with choosing my
lover

God Must Be A Black Woman

God must be a Black Woman
Cause only a Black Woman can put up with all the shit
men give them
Now I'm not going to exclude myself from this
conversation
I've been known to be reckless and dangerous
But God still working-
Excuse me,
My Black Woman is still working on me
We can often be stuck in our ways but just like God
Our Black Women can set us straight
Set us on the correct path to righteousness
Open our third eye of consciousness
Cause every time she makes me climax
I see, GOD
Well I see, HER
Lying next to me so elegantly
I never knew I could experience this kind of divinity
While sharing an embrace of serenity
Am I dreaming or living in ecstasy
In a King size bed with this Ebony Queen surrounding
me
Using her powers of empathy devouring my every
insecurity
Loving me unconditionally and endlessly
And creating my legacy as I plant my seed of destiny
Ultimately giving my last name longevity
God Must Be A Black Woman
Cause I'm writing poetry about the most hated and
loved woman in the world
For every Black Woman breastfeeding the universe

Giving us her nutrients, her body, her mind, spirit, and
soul
I love how her energy grows and powers our world
I guess God wants me to write about every Black Girl
Manifesting realities of different sizes while rocking her
natural curls
She's killing me softly and loving me dangerously
Black Women are Godly!

A Winter Kiss

I met her in the middle of Winter, I think it was the coldest day in December. The coldest Winter I've ever endured was when she kissed me the first time. She had the ability to command my presence if needed. Even though there was evil present in the Garden of Eden I still would've eaten anything she decided. The forbidden fruit she provided had me excited for my survival. A Winter kiss so deep I felt the color of her velvet lips. With her moist flesh pressed against mine we began tossing and turning for a lifetime. This was her way of saying I love you, but I'm only here temporarily. Even though she was my everything momentarily. And I find it quite extraordinary that she would make me her priority only for a moment of physical therapy; while I'm stuck in curiosity wondering who decided to give her the authority to lead me into a world of inconsistency. But that first Winter kiss will be one I will always miss. I guess I'll just have to reminisce on that old bliss.

Walls Hold Memories

My Father and my best friend both passed away suddenly and the one thing that bothers me the most is that I can still hear their voices, so I turn around to see if their still there and it's nothing but air. It's like their voices are Ghosts of Christmas past and I can still hear the way they laugh. Death happens suddenly, without warning or introduction. It's like knocking on a door of an empty home. The walls hold memories, the mirrors tell stories and every time I hear them, I wish they can hear me. That's just bittersweet poetry.

Phantom Prisoner

Everywhere I went she was the phantom of my dreams
The unseen wind that blew through my body sending
winter chills up my spine
Our first kiss was between two strangers
Two hearts beating as one in a world full of danger

A Kiss Like This

My temperature rising from kissing on her flesh
This feeling I can't resist
now we're tasting what each other has to offer
Embracing our own insecurities
And replacing them with sensuality
Hoping we won't become a liability
While we encourage each other's sexual fantasies
She never had her thighs spread so wide
She's never been kissed like this
While my tongue preceded to perform gymnastics from
East to West
She used both of her hands
And grabbed the back of my head and pushed me in
Deeper
Moaning
"Baby it's the best"
I gave her oral pleasure From
East to West
Treating her body like it was new lands to be
discovered I didn't want to rush
I took my time trying to discover this woman's buried
Treasure
Cause I know sometimes it takes patience in order to
Master Pleasure
So, I gave her exactly what she needed
Just a little pressure
Pure stimulating
Perfectly executed
And proudly reciprocated
She couldn't control her reactions
She tried to run away

The pleasure was beginning to be too much
So, I put her legs on my shoulders
grabbed her by the hips
And pulled her in closer
I wanted to finish what I was doing
In order to give her body some closure
And when it was all over
We shared our final kiss
One I will always miss
she bit my bottom lip
And I just couldn't resist
Tasting a black woman like this!

Naked

What's your favorite position
Is it face to face or are your feelings just a place for
mistakes
Tell me when did loving someone become such a
burden
Tell me, have you ever been naked before
I don't mean shirtless but open-hearted
I don't mean nude but possibly in an open mood
Open to your emotions and dreams
Have you had conversations on your what if's or
maybe's
What happens when you try to let someone in
And how many times have you tried
Have you ever made love under 1000 suns
And have you ever thought if they were the one
Have you ever counted the stars in the night sky
Have you ever wondered why lovers lie
Have you ever been naked before

The Outside

I was outside smoking a stogie with the homies when my homie got a call from Brittany saying she wasn't feeling to easy. She said she was pregnant with his baby and he wasn't ready for that type of responsibility. So, he felt abortion was his only option. He felt his other obligations were slightly more important than their creation. She's prolife, while my homie thinking about his pockets, he's prochoice. So, she called me later on and we were talking on the phone saying your homeboy want to act like he all grown but when the time comes, he can't man up, why the hell you put me on? And I feel slightly responsible I introduced them into each other, but how was I to know that he wasn't man enough to be your baby's Father. I figured he would've made better decisions and wore protection, how was I supposed to know y'all didn't have that kind of connection? I guess actions have repercussions. And now this baby doesn't have a say so because one parent is a no show and the other is on the outside. Trying to hold on to her pride thinking she can raise this baby on her own if she has to, but she really wants the baby's Father to be there too. So, what's a Mother to do when she's forced to be a single parent instead of two. She's stuck on the outside looking in.

October 16

It was just a regular day at the office. I was ready to go home, and I didn't really feel like being bothered that day like most days at work. And then I got a missed call from your brother. And one turned into two then I got a text. "Call me when you get a chance." So, I did. And even though I knew you were sick and even though I had a gut feeling of what came next I didn't want to believe it. My best friend had passed away. And all I could say is why God? Not him. Not today. Not like this. We were supposed to get rich and famous together. We were supposed to talk about all the crazy people in this world together and now it just seems like I'm stuck in stormy weather. I still can't believe your gone. And I really hate that you had to leave so soon. So, I tell myself you're in a better place. But what does that mean for me? What does that mean for the people you left behind. If you're in a better place does that mean my current situation is worse? Help me understand, how can family and friends being happy together and when one leaves, we assume their happiness is away from us. They receive happiness in death, so we stuck with memories of ghosts. How am I supposed to be satisfied that my best friend died, and I had no say in the matter? Am I supposed to suck it up, stop crying and be grateful for the time we had together. I just want my homie back. Talk about anime and all the Marvel movies that's coming out. How Disney has literally taken over everything and when I mean everything, I mean everything. Too bad my friend didn't get the Disney or Fairytale ending. So, I wrote this poem for him instead. So, he'll always be remembered. He'll always be the one friend I could count on, but damn I just wish he was here, just one more time to tell a joke and make us all laugh. October 16th, a day I wish we could all just pass.

Remembering 2018

For me, I'll always remember 2018
That was the year my son was born
The light of my world
And later that year my best friend passed away
A day I thought would never happen
Two things on different sides of the spectrum
Happened in the same year
I became a Father and a Mourner
2018 gave me all kinds of emotions
That year happened so fast

Love Life and Regrets

My biggest regret is that I didn't fall in love sooner
Allow me to rephrase
My biggest regret is that I didn't love her better
My biggest regret is that I'll see her in love with another
My biggest regret is that I broke her heart
And it seems like all things fall apart
Correction
It seems like I grew apart from her
My biggest regret is that I'll never know what love is
Actually
I'll never know what I meant to her
She loved me for who I was
Or at least who I am at that time
Which in hindsight meant everything to her
I didn't love her the way she loved me
I mean
I couldn't love her because love wasn't in me
And now that she's gone away from me
My biggest regret is that I didn't fall in love sooner
Allow me to rephrase
My biggest regret is that I didn't love her better
She had the audacity to love me
And I had the insanity not to reciprocate
I can't believe I was that stupid
Correction
How could I be so ignorant to love and understand

Matthew 7:15

I wish you realized that I wasn't shit to begin with
I wish that you didn't waste your time and fill your heart
and mind with a thousand of my lies
For you to sit and hang on to every false seed I sowed
into you
And for that hatred to grow into a tree of uncertainty
I wish you had chosen not to fall in love with me
Cause all I did was break your heart into a million
pieces
And turned what was a beautiful black woman into a
damaged version of her former self
I was your demise
And all those nights I heard your cries
Your tears baptized my pillows and clouded your skies
I allowed you to be hypnotized by my scripture
While you prayed for the salvation, I never delivered
you from
I sincerely apologize for my negligence
I never intended to become the Bishop of your
maleficence
You were never the burden that you had to carry
The cross you held on your back were only my sins to
carry.

While You Were Sleeping

While you were sleeping, I counted every eyelash on both of your eyes twice. While you were sleeping, I counted every freckle upon your face and on the outside looking in, you would've thought I was a psycho. But on the contrary, I'm in love. I watch you when you sleep so I can protect you from those bad dreams so when you wake up from your nightmares, I'll be there to comfort you in the real world. The world can be a scary place and the dreams we have may even be worse but while you were sleeping, I was out conquering the world.

I was slaying a thousand dragons, exercising genocidal demons, curing incurable diseases, healing pains of emotional and physical abuse, trying to make this world a better place for you. While you were sleeping, I made several mistakes. Trying to become a better me for a better you only to realize that how I was, is more than enough for you. While you were sleeping, I cried. I cried thinking maybe I'm not good enough so I try to save you, protect you, keep you all to myself so that no one will try to hurt you. Because I know how it feels.

I know how it feels to be alone in the dark with a room full of people.

While you were sleeping, I tried to live for you instead of living for me.

The Grace

I don't want a quick fuck
I want something real
And I know, I know I'm a man and all
But when I'm trying to go deeper
I'm searching for a connection,
Not just a one-night stand
I'm looking for something that's going to stay
I need something that's not gonna leave when I'm
finished
something that's going to love me in return when I finish
I want something more than just a one-night stand
I'm searching for commitment
Something that's gonna last forever
And I know I'm gonna treat that body right
And discover new places while you tell me your pussy
tight
Too hot to handle too tight to manage
As I think of ways to be your erotic savage
I want to be resurrected in your wetness
Drown me in your orgasms
Become baptized by your holy waters
And drink from your golden chalice
I want to say Grace
As I enjoy you as my Last Supper
Get on my hands and knees and worship
While I do sinful things to you

<u>Chase Your Dreams</u>

It's ok to go after your desires if it pleases you
It's ok to taste the rivers of the world and spit out the
unnecessary and uncertainty.
You should be able to swallow your fears and gain the
strength and knowledge of your ancestor's tears.
I am with you.
I encourage you to discover who you are no matter how
you must do it.
If that means digging up the past or removing skeletons
from a damaged and broken closet that was locked up
years ago.
If that means you have to show your self-inflicted scars
that could have killed, you.
I implore you to live your best life.
Become the better you the mirror stares into.

Sacred

Can I kiss you in the most sacred of places
While I thank God for your Grace
As we lay in our final embrace
I want to make it known this is no mistake
This is something sacred
You are the world's greatest treasure
And just for that I am grateful for your glory

Names and Things

I feel that names and titles complicate things
So, let's not put a title on what we have
Let's just do what we do
No one has to know what's between us
It's not for the world to know
So, let's continue our affair
If that's what you want to call it
Names and things

A Love Like

I love her, but I also love me more
I want her, but I also want to be free
I want to keep her, but I'm afraid of losing it all
I want to make love
But I've never done that before
I want a love like R&B
But I'm not sure I know what that means
I want to be sure that she is the one for me
But I'm afraid to take that chance
I'm not cut out for rejections
Just pure romance
All I know is pain can cause reflections
And heartache don't come with medicine
There's no Doctor or over the counter prescriptions
Some people love with no reason
But I know I want passion
I'm a hopeless romantic
And when it comes to love I'm at a disadvantage
I'm a loner in a world full of companions
Love conquers all
But I'm no champion
I love her
But I love me more now
There was a time when I didn't know how
I had to learn to love the skin I'm in
So, I can love her later
So, I can love her better
So, I can love her forever

Preventing The Inevitable

I'm afraid of two things
Failure and Death
And I know one of those things are inevitable
I don't want to die, and I don't want to fail in life either
How can I cheat death without being a failure
This life is full of pressure
With no escape for the inevitable

The Secrets We Keep and The Lies We Speak

I wonder if your boyfriend told you all his secrets would
you still love him
I wonder if I told you all of mine would you still stand
next to me
It's interesting the secrets we keep from each other not
knowing the hurt or damage of them
Does hiding your skeletons make you safe or selfish
If these walls could talk the conversations would be
endless
And if the mirror could whisper the truth, oh my, my,
my,
Tell the truth and shame the Devil
But Lucifer never told a lie
So, if you were to ask a fallen Angel where the truth
lies, would you ask him
Or would you pray to God for the truth
What hurts more facts or fiction
If it's beyond belief, then why do we understand fiction
Think about the secrets you keep
Do you dream about the truth you wish you could speak

A Lover's Existence

The next time we make love keep your eyes open, so I
know it's real!
Don't close your eyes no matter how good it feels!
I want to stare into your soul with every stroke
And stimulate every Chakra and have an out-of-body
experience
So, we can meet God together
I want to feel your heartbeat faster
While I listen to your breath get deeper as we both
climax into oblivion.

Choke Me

Have you ever been choked before?
No?
Me either
But for some reason I want my wife to reach up and choke me while we're making love
Now I have never been in an abusive relationship before and I don't even know if I'm into some weird fetish but there's something that makes me curious as to want to be choked.
Like I want to be on top while we're making love and we're making deep eye contact while I'm penetrating her she's penetrating my soul and before I began to lose myself she reaches up to choke me to let me know she's in control. You see it's not about the actual choke or the stroke but the ability to give her control! I need to be choked. Choke me so I know it's real. Squeeze my neck harder so I know the pain you feel. Choke me harder so I can stay in check. Don't be afraid to break my neck just be affirmative that this love thing is best.
I told her to choke me, so I know it's real!
Choke me
so, I know it's real
Scream my name
so, I know this pleasure is a new feel
Squeeze tighter
So, I know this passion is hard like steel
Choke me
So, I know you're in control
Look into my eyes
Stare into my soul
And don't ever let me go

So, call my phone
Like a psycho
Hold me tight
So, I can't let go
Worship me
Like the God you pray to
And hurt me like the Devil told you
I need you to choke me!

Press Pause on Love

If you fall in love today and tomorrow you were
heartbroken,
Would you want to repeat today?
What if you can skip to the exact day you were to fall in
love?
Not knowing if it would turn into a tragic end.
Would you rewind time to fall in love over and over
again?
If I could press pause on love and live in the moment
I would.
But would that be considered a bad omen?
If you can't learn from your mistakes and only here for
the good moments
how do you enjoy the sunshine when you don't
know rain?
So you really can't enjoy love if can't remember pain.
You can't miss anything you never had.
Can you?
Your tears won't flow if your heart is always on the go.
So if you were asked to press pause on love.
Would you?
If it's better to have loved and lost than not have loved
at all
Then at my highest moment of love I'll press pause
And relive that moment every single day
I'm so tired of pain
So I'll stay stuck in love any day.

<u>Diamond In The Ruff</u>

For every Black Mother that had to raise a child on her
own
I hear you
I see you
And most importantly I love you
You are not forgotten
We treasure you
For every Black woman who has their back against the
wall
I'm with you
For every Black girl who can't find a way out
I'll find you
For every Black girl who is in a dark place
I'll try my best to light your way
For every Black Woman
For every Black Girl in this world
I am with you.

Lost Love

When you fall in love for the umpteenth time what
makes this one different
When that same guy turns your heart into broken
pieces of glass
After you've had fifteen shots from your Grandad's old
flask
And now you wear depression like a hero's mask
Your secret identity is pain
So your archvillain is self
No "S" on your chest
Cause the one person you can't save is yourself
Tell me love
What makes a good lover
What makes your heart want to be a giver
Not everyone deserves the love you give
Hold on to what you know is real
These fools don't deserve your time
Just comic book characters searching for a good rhyme

Appetizer

She asked me what's your favorite fruit
I replied whatever you taste like
She smiled and said oh is that right
You've tasted the forbidden fruit
Yes, love, I'm a connoisseur of all God's treasures
And so I love to taste everything, simply for your
pleasure

One Thousand Thoughts of Love

When I'm alone with you I try to think of a thousand
ways to love you better
With every hug I try to hold you just a little tighter
A little longer
More than enough to set your soul on fire
Every kiss a little deeper
Just to make it that much sweeter
Often, I think about your perspective
How does she see me
And if I'm everything she wants and more
I have a thousand dreams of us sharing different
realities
Where we live as Royalty with seven kingdoms
One where we have children by the dozens
We'll be worshiped like Gods and live on for eons
And name our Generations after the stars
So all our people will flourish from one thousand
thoughts of love

Pyramids

I met a girl named Egypt
I've always wanted to go there
Staring at the pyramid between her thighs
I imagined exploring her Cairo
And other places no other man dared to go
My Egyptian Queen
My Nefertiti
Allow me to worship you like royalty
And the sands of time will carry our love
For all eternity

Escucha Eros

I've been praying to God for 31 years
And the 1st time I heard him talk back was when I saw
you
He said here I made her for you
All you have to do is
Listen
Love
Learn
Honor
Protect
Cherish
Commit
-and Encourage her

Glass Half Empty

I just want to live forever in a world that's not promised
tomorrow
I'm so tired of singing sorrows
My time feels borrowed
If I were to fall in love today,
I'd be pissed, cause I might die tomorrow
I got all this love to give and can't get over yesterday's
sorrow
My time feels borrowed
I'm running with the Devil cause the Angels won't follow
My demons keep me company
So I'm only lonely when I'm in the presence of my
family
Damn
I'm the perfect tragedy
My own worst enemy
Battling the Demons that still live in me
And questioning the Blessings bestowed upon me

<u>Mind Battle</u>

Sometimes I wonder if I'm good enough
If I'm man enough
Sometimes I feel like I'm not enough for you
And it bothers me because in my mind I am
But Sometimes I feel like I'm just not the one
Feel free to correct me if I'm wrong but are you happy
or not
These are Just feelings I have when I'm alone with my
thoughts

Five More

I wish I had just five more minutes to talk to my loved ones
Just one more drink
One more game
One more laugh
One more meal
And one less time to heal
Why can't my loved ones just stay here
No more tears
No more fears
Why does death have to follow me here

Something In Between

I often think of you when I'm with her
And I'm not sure if that makes me a bad person or not
I guess it's just bad timing
God usually gives you the one you need
Not the one you want
Maybe we were lovers in another life
It just so happens we were both reincarnated at the same time
Unfortunately, we meet again unable to love each other
Star crossed lovers who may have been destined to be together
That's what happens when love doesn't die it just lives on
Like something in between

Changing Situations

I heard you don't get naughty for anybody
So does that mean I'm a somebody
Cause lately you've been acting kind of shady
Behaving strangely and nonchalantly
No love just odd melancholy

4 Play

Seduction is the perfect appetizer to foreplay
I need BOTH
I'll be the perfect host
Your body is the main course
A dish so delicate I can still taste you while I sleep
Some see seduction as art
I see it as fine cuisine
I'll indulge myself into your spirit
As I lick your plate clean
Allow me to caress your body
Don't keep biting your lip
When what I want you to do is bite mine
I want to consume every piece of you
Until I taste the flavor of your mind
I'll be patient
And I'll be kind
I want all of your body
So I can take my time
Unbutton your dress one button at a time
Kisses on your neck like war crimes
My lips massaging the tension down your spine
Patiently
Passionately
Precisely
Foreplay is only the beginning

BBW

Beautiful Black Women
I think every man has a preference whether he admits it
or not
I think every man desires a taste like hers whether he's
thirsty or not
And if its a thirst quench I desire
I'm prepared to drown in your waters
And if this is a sin that I speak then baptize me in the
fire
Damn my soul for eternity
While I lay in your bosom of serenity
For I have been resurrected in your secret garden
A genesis of erotic obsession
I want to touch you in the most sacred of places
And watch you make strong orgasmic faces
Witnessing you reach the highest plateau of satisfaction
Can't nobody like me give you that type of gratification
I want to discover every curve your body has to offer
In efforts to learn what your body truly desires
I want to drink from your lips while both of my hands are
gently massaging your hips
And feel the warmth of your inner thighs against my
cheeks
As you squeeze them tighter by uncontrollable oral
pleasure
Climax
Your body trembles beneath me
Your hands grab the sheets tightly
Your eyes roll to the back of your head drastically
You scream my name passionately
Beautiful

Black
Woman
Love me tenderly
Treat me kindly
Cherish our memories
Sex me crazy
Encourage me firmly
And I will worship you
For all eternity

Skin Deep

I heard there was an African American studies class
being taught in school
But the attendance was low
And they say history repeats itself, so I guess now we
enslaving ourselves
I assume my generation isn't concerned with history
just the present and the not so distant future
My homeboy asked me what happened to hip-hop
And I told him niggas stop writing poetry
More focused on drinking lean
And smoking weed
It's a whole lot of young crack fiends
So what happened to hip-hop?
Same thing that happens to everything else I guess
The white man came in and pimped us out
Promising fast money, women, fashion and gold chains
Like they ancestors weren't chained like savages
Held together in bondage
And want to pretend like our skin don't have knowledge
I guess the Negro Spirituals your Grandma sang ain't
Dark Skin enough
Maybe her slave masters whip not strong enough
Are your Grandfather's tears not wet enough
Don't you remember the stories of our ancestors
hanging lifeless from bloody trees
And injustices that never seem to leave
Why the hell we still getting shot by the police
What happened to hip-hop
You think the revolution is over
You must think you free
What's a free man to sold world

Oh so you came from a wealthy family tree
And on top of that you got a few college degrees
You might make more money than the homies in your group
Just to get pulled over by the cops and you still a nigga in a coupe
Don't worry about it
Put your damn hands up
They won't shoot
Your skin dark enough for them to think first then execute
It's Skin Deep
And the bodies of our black history lay under our feet
When our Queens are being snatched in the street
And our Kings get gunned down every time we speak
Class is now in session
Will you be in attendance

Which Are You

Desperate times call for desperate measures
Do you follow your passion or are you tempted by pleasure
What type of secrets do you treasure
Not every consequence has pressure
Are you a student or professor
Who is your oppressor
Can you identify your savior?

Dark Chocolate

A love like hers is bittersweet
But maybe I had to many drinks at the bar
And I'm getting dizzy
Arguments over petty little things
But the love we make can conquer anything
Every fight is worthwhile
And I'll be willing to go into exile
They'll probably rewrite Dante's Inferno after me
My story of Hell and Her
Or the Hell she puts me through
Perhaps,
Maybe the Hell I put her through
Maybe we are each other's Hell
Whenever we're not making each other visit Heaven
We can make each other see God with a simple kiss
And we also can make ourselves monsters
Disguised as ordinary people
We are the calm before the storm
Dark Chocolate has an acquired taste
And it's one I can never escape
She's got a hold on me
And I have a vampiric thirst for her
A bond stronger than any curse
Its Witchcraft
She's a spiritual being
She is all I'll ever need
She's Dark Chocolate
She's Bittersweet
An acquired taste
Someone I'll forever appreciate

The Love Kiss

She kissed me and said I love you
And I was shocked because I love her too
but I didn't want to say it first
Too afraid that maybe she might not feel the same way
And my heart wasn't prepared for that type of rejection
I was willing to accept being with her for eternity
Not knowing if she actually loved me
And I was ok with that
Call me crazy but I knew what I had,
and I was afraid of losing it
People say you don't know what you've got till it's gone
but I knew what I had, and I didn't want it to leave
I have a fear of jeopardizing the unknown
Especially if I feel that something is right
I didn't want to lose what I had in sight
Everything felt so proper
The way it should be
I still get butterflies trying to plan her little surprises
And I still think of ways to love her better than the day
before
I literally worry about if she loves me the way she used
to
I'm not perfect myself I do have flaws
but being in love with her just keeps me in awe
I've watched her sleep like a psychopath hoping I can
enter her dreams and live forever
I want to make love to her repeatedly because her body
just isn't enough
I want every part of her mind, body, and soul

I want her to have all my children and hope their children's children remember her and love her just as much as I do

The Sweet Life

Late nights on the beach until the moon kisses the water and the sun peaks from beneath The sweetest of fruits are only as sweet as the life you live. But sometimes bitterness and sour flavors can ruin even the sweetest of melons. When life gives you lemons you make lemonade but with no sugar, so your drink is still bitter. The Sweet Life isn't so sweet when she reminds you of stress. Dreams don't become a reality if there's no one sleeping. Coffee doesn't taste the same when you're heartbroken. The Sweet Life is only sweet after the rain falls.

Desperate For Affection

Have you ever been so desperate for affection
I'm talking about have you ever been tired of rejection
And have you ever been afraid of natural selection
Suggesting that maybe you're better off alone. Or
maybe that special someone just hasn't come home
Maybe they will or maybe they won't

The Thrill

Your husband called my phone and asked me what I
was doing with his wife
I guess I didn't get the memo that you belonged to
someone else
How heartbroken he must've been
Knowing his wife was my little plaything
I wondered how he found out
And what his immediate reaction was
He probably called you several expletives
And everything else under the Sun but a child of God.
But can you blame him
I've undressed your blouse at least 1000 times
I've penetrated your mind, body, and soul
And you still can't seem to get enough
We've been doing this every Sunday through Thursday
And now I know how you spend your weekends.
You're with him on the days you're not with me
And the fact that you never denied it only tells me one
thing
You like it
It's either you want to be caught
Or
You like The Thrill
You like the fact that I'm your weekend flavor
And I like the fact that you can't get enough of it either
So, the next time you're with him
Tell him how you like to be tied up
Tell him you like blindfolds
Tell him how you liked to be choked
Tell him you just can't get enough
And tell him he just ain't got the right stuff

So, what will you tell him
That I make your body shake
How I use my tongue to make you cum
Perhaps how I kiss you ear to ear
As your eyes produce orgasmic tears
That I've explored every part of your body and your
husband wouldn't recognize your passionate cries
Would you be mad if I told him she doesn't belong to
you anymore?
She never did
She's mine now
Ask her the next time you see her
The Thrill has taken over her

Love and the High School Dilemma

I think I love girls too much
And the problem with that is do they love me back
I don't think I have an issue with love
Maybe just the ones I choose to fall in love with
I have a dilemma on my hands
And my heart can't seem to grasp it
My brain refuses to acknowledge it and my soul...
My soul just wants to be happy
But what's happiness to a broken heart
What's a man to do when all things fall apart
I have a dilemma
I'm a hopeless romantic
So that makes me vulnerable
It makes me say and do things I don't mean
Even when I think I mean them
My emotions are playing a game of tug of war
With her on the other side
And she's the strongest girl in the whole school
And my fingers are slipping
All while another girl I admire is watching my downfall
She watches me run late for class while hers is down
the hall
I try to catch my breath, but I lost my inhaler
And every time I pass by her I try to inhale her
Cause the air she carries smell like Cherry Blossoms
Which is probably why I'm failing Chemistry
And I've probably committed more sins in my ministry
But that's neither here nor there, so let's just call it
history
Hopefully it won't repeat itself
I'll possibly find a way to redeem myself

But my problem is I love girls too much.

All A Man Needs

All a man really needs is the love of his wife
And the smile of his children
Because material things become obsolete and when
your family is everything
You will have the strength and courage to do anything

Priceless

If a man sells his soul to live forever, he'll live the rest of his life trying to die
So why waste your time chasing a dollar instead of a dream
When the money runs out and your digging into the seams
Because those materialistic things aren't what they seem
And that girl you met on the block, well she just a money fiend
Trying to persuade you into empty things and now you're a ghost in the machine.

Worthwhile

When a man finds the love of his life
Nothing in the world matters
His problems disappear every time she smiles
Making his life worthwhile
The world is only enough with her in it
She will be his everything

Love-Less

A man can't love a woman when he don't love himself
So, how can you love a selfish man
It's hard to love someone when love don't love you
back

Timeless

All the money in the world can't buy a love like hers
But a love like hers can buy all the time I have to give
I would give all the years of my life
Just to spend another day with my wife

<u>Be Still</u>

Even when you're angry
Learn to be still
Too often we make mistakes
Because we moved in our anger
We make split second decisions
Never focusing on the consequences
It's essential we learn how our words have dangerous
potential

Talking To Ghosts

Ever since I was a child, I would always talk to myself. I would never get a reply just holding conversations with air, I guess. Maybe I was teaching myself how to cope with stress or find some way of escape. I believe now my younger self was teaching me how to deal with death.

When I was at my best friends' funeral, I couldn't believe he was there laying in box. This decorated coffin will now be buried along with all his thoughts. And I remember specifically as they closed the top of his casket, I was having a full-blown conversation. My mind was racing, and I couldn't get it to stop. I was talking to my best friends' ghost and I didn't even know it. Conversations to go along with loneliness and the voices don't stop. I tell people all the time I can still hear his voice. I'm talking to ghosts and they were taking notes. It's like a party for the dead is all in my head and I was the perfect host.

A Melanated King

I was born under the sun
So my skin reflects it
My ancestors had magic in their veins
So I bleed Royalty
And everything I touch turns to gold
They used to call it alchemy
Maybe I just have the Midas Touch
But in reality
I'm a Melanated King
How's that for society
This Black Boy with all this Black Boy Joy
The Black Prince with glory in the mix
This Black King who walks with Black Ancestors that
Sing
The Black Man that treats his Black Queen like Kings in
Chess
The only way to end this poem is for my all my Black
Queens to say yes!
To a Melanated King!

THE
END

THE

END